True.   _Very true._

❧ Dear Reader,

If you read the Old Testament of the Holy Bible, you will
find that it is packed full of brilliant and exciting stories.
In this book I have chosen my favourites. They are:

GOD'S CREATIONS ✳ page 6

THE GARDEN OF EDEN ✳ page 8

NOAH'S ARK ✳ page 10

ABRAHAM AND ISAAC ✳ page 14

JOSEPH AND HIS FABULOUS ROBE ✳ page 16

THE STORY OF MOSES ✳ page 20

THE BATTLE OF JERICHO ✳ page 24

SAMSON AND DELILAH ✳ page 26

DAVID AND GOLIATH ✳ page 28

DANIEL IN THE LIONS' DEN ✳ page 30

JONAH AND THE GREAT FISH ✳ page 34

I have spent many happy hours retelling and illustrating
these stories and I hope they will give you many happy
hours of reading and looking.

❧ _Marcia Williams_

_They are
simply divine!_

P.S. The words spoken by God are taken from the New International
Version of the Bible. All the others are my own, inspired by reading this version.

First published 2004 by Walker Books Ltd
87 Vauxhall Walk, London SE11 5HJ

This edition published 2005

10 9 8 7 6 5 4 3 2 1

© 2004 Marcia Williams

The right of Marcia Williams to be identified as
author/illustrator of this work has been asserted by her
in accordance with the Copyright, Designs and Patents Act 1988

This book has been typeset in Phaistos Bold

Printed in China

British Library Cataloguing in Publication Data: a catalogue record
for this book is available from the British Library

ISBN 1-84428-528-6

www.walkerbooks.co.uk

For Oscar, Hettie and Albert, with love

GOD
AND HIS
CREATIONS

Tales from the Old Testament

Retold and illustrated by

Marcia Williams

WALKER BOOKS
AND SUBSIDIARIES
LONDON · BOSTON · SYDNEY · AUCKLAND

GOD'S CREATIONS

In the beginning there was only God. The earth was formless and dark.

Then God created light! He called the light "day", and the darkness "night" – on that first day.

On the second day God created space to divide the waters. He called it "sky".

On the third day God made rivers, seas, and dry land that was rich in plants and trees.

God put the sun, the moon and the stars in the sky.
So there was evening, and there was morning – on that fourth day.

On the fifth day God filled the seas with fish, and the sky with insects and birds.
He loved each and every one.

On the sixth day God was very busy.
He made animals of every shape and size to live upon the land.

Then, out of the dust of the earth, God made men and women.
He made them to care for the earth and for all living creatures.

God saw all that He had made and it was very good. In six days He had created
the whole world, so He made the seventh day a rest day.

Genesis

THE GARDEN OF EDEN

The first man God breathed life into was Adam. God planted a garden called Eden for Adam to live in. God told Adam to enjoy all the fruits of Eden, except for those from the tree of the knowledge of good and evil — for if he tasted these, he would die. Adam obeyed God, for he loved Him. But when God was not with him in the garden, Adam felt lonely.

NOAH'S ARK

Then God told Noah to fill the ark with a male and female of every living creature. So he and his family chased, herded and coaxed until the ark was loaded. As the first drops of rain began to fall, God slammed the great door shut and bolted it firmly.

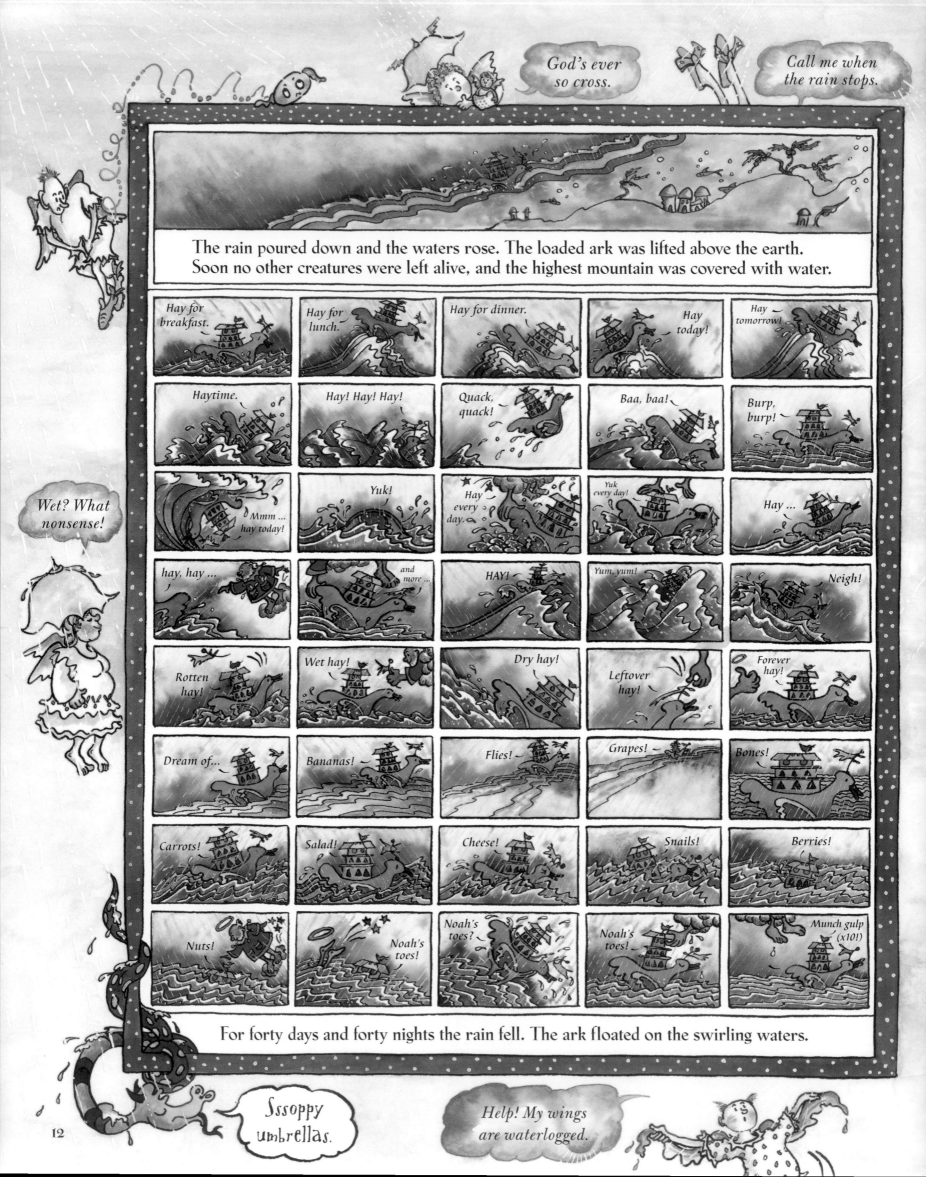

Until at last God sent a wind over the earth. The rain ceased and the waters began to recede.

The ark came to rest on Mt Ararat. Noah let out a raven, but it found nowhere to land.

A few days later Noah sent out a dove. It flew for miles, but could find nowhere to rest its feet.

Seven days later Noah sent out the dove again. In the evening it returned with an olive branch.

After another seven days the dove flew out again. It did not return, because the earth had dried.

Their hay-days are over.

Noah opened the great doors of the ark and out rushed his family and all God's creatures. Noah built an altar to thank God, and God was delighted. He promised Noah never to flood the world again, and He set a rainbow in the sky as a sign of His promise.

Genesis

What a wet tale.

ABRAHAM AND ISAAC

After Noah, there was a shepherd named Abraham who loved God above everything else. When God asked him to travel to Canaan with his wife Sarah, he did not hesitate.

When they reached Canaan, God visited them again.

He told Abraham and Sarah that they would have a son.

They laughed, thinking they were too old to have a child.

But the next year, as God had said, Sarah gave birth to a boy.

They named him Isaac and he grew healthy and strong.

Abraham and Sarah were very proud; they loved Isaac dearly.

So when God asked Abraham to sacrifice Isaac as a burnt offering, Abraham thought his heart would break. But he collected wood, some fire and a sacrificial knife and set out with his son.

After three days Abraham and Isaac reached the place that God had chosen for the sacrifice.

Abraham bound Isaac and placed him on top of an altar. But, as he raised the knife, an angel stopped him. God had been testing Abraham and now He was sure that Abraham loved Him above all else. God promised Abraham that his descendants would be leaders of great nations.

Abraham and Isaac returned joyfully home to Canaan to tell Sarah of God's great promise.

Genesis

15

What about new wings for me?

Twelve boys – what perfection!

God's had a hand in this.

Sweet dreams!

I remember when you were a boy, Isaac.

Dad, Gramps, I've brought the boys to see you.

Isaac, the son of Abraham, stayed in Canaan and had twin sons of his own, Esau and Jacob. Jacob became a farmer and had twelve sons.

That's my boy!

It's fab! Thanks, Dad.

It stinks!

Jacob loved his sons, but especially Joseph. He gave him a new robe. Joseph's brothers were jealous and began to hate him.

Then Joseph had two strange dreams. In the first, Joseph and his brothers were binding corn.

Suddenly Joseph's sheaf rose and stood upright and his brothers' sheaves bowed down before it.

In the second dream the sun, the moon and eleven stars bowed down before him as though he were king.

We must keep this matter in mind, my dearest boy!

He thinks he'll actually rule us. No chance – baa!

His father believed the dreams meant that Joseph would become a ruler. His brothers' hatred grew. They stormed off to tend the sheep.

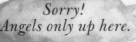
Sorry! Angels only up here.

You're my favourite doll.

16

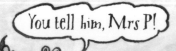

God likes
long-term plans.

In Egypt Joseph was sold as a slave to Potiphar, the captain of Pharaoh's guard.

You are promoted – you now care for the whole household!

Great!

You may please Potiphar, but you don't please me.

Big mistake!

Joseph, what do dead rats dream about?

God knows!

For a while Joseph did well as a slave.

But then Potiphar's wife had him thrown into prison.

In prison Joseph became a wise interpreter of dreams.

God will help Joseph.

Bring that Joseph fellow.

OK, mighty Pharaoh.

You stink!

You stink to high heaven!

Can you help?

God willing.

So when Pharaoh had two strange dreams, he called upon Joseph to interpret them.

In the first dream, seven sleek, fat cows came out of the River Nile, followed by seven scrawny, gaunt cows. The scrawny, gaunt cows ate the sleek, fat cows but remained thin.

Those are bad dreams!

Grrr!

Crunch!

Help!

Slurp!

Burp!

Fat is not fun!

In his second dream, seven shrivelled ears of corn swallowed up seven fat ears of corn.

This matter is firmly decided … listen!

You must collect grain during the seven good years.

Since God has made this known to you, you're in charge.

He needs a haircut.

Great!

Joseph told Pharaoh that God had sent him a warning: seven years of plenty would be followed by seven years of famine!

Pharaoh was so impressed by Joseph's wisdom that he put him in charge of storing food for the famine to come.

Famine is forbidden in heaven.

Luckily for you!

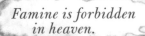
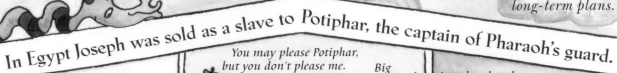

THE STORY OF MOSES

 Your name will be Israel.

 A new name at my age – what next!

Before Jacob died, God changed his name to Israel, and his descendants – Joseph and his brothers, and their children, and their children's children – became known as the Israelites.

Poor, lonely baby.

The Israelites have become too numerous. Make them slaves.

Good plan, mighty Pharaoh.

When they give birth, if it's a boy, kill him!

Even better plan, mighty Pharaoh.

The Israelites became so rich and numerous in Egypt that the Pharaoh began to fear their power. He made them slaves, and ordered the death of all their baby boys.

Yummy fish!

 This must be an Israelite baby.

To save her son, one Israelite mother hid her baby among the reeds by the bank of the Nile. Pharaoh's daughter found him there when she came to bathe. She named the baby Moses and took him home to live with her as her son.

God must have plans for Moses.

 Stop that.

Carry the whole pyramid, not just one brick!

 Run, Moses, or Daddy will kill you!

I'm out of here!

Moses knew that his parents were Israelites, and, as he grew older, he tried to protect other Israelites. One day he killed an Egyptian for giving an Israelite slave a cruel beating, and so he was forced to flee from Egypt.

Know-all!

*I hope his luck holds out.*

Far away from Pharaoh's wrath Moses found work as a shepherd. But God had a job for him.

Who am I? Why would Pharaoh listen to me?

I will be with you.

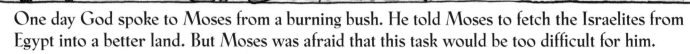

One day God spoke to Moses from a burning bush. He told Moses to fetch the Israelites from Egypt into a better land. But Moses was afraid that this task would be too difficult for him.

Grrrr.

Gulp!

God told Moses to throw down his staff. It became a snake.

When God told Moses to pick the snake up by the tail, it became a staff again.

God told Moses to put his hand inside his cloak. His hand turned sickly white.

When he replaced his hand inside his cloak, it was healed.

Bother, bother, bother, bother!

I still think God should send some other poor soul!

Me too!

God said signs like these would convince Pharaoh to let the Israelites go. He told Moses not to be afraid. At last Moses obeyed, and set out for Egypt with the staff of God in his hand.

Yoo-hoo! Moses, I've made a map!

EGYPT FROM THE SKY

In Egypt Moses asked Pharaoh to release the Israelites. He showed God's signs with his staff.

But Pharaoh would not listen. So God sent plagues, as more signs, to persuade him.

God turned all the water of Egypt into blood.

He made a plague of frogs hop across the land.

He turned the dust of Egypt into gnats.

He sent swarms of big, buzzing flies.

He visited a terrible disease upon all Egyptian animals.

He tortured the Egyptian people with festering boils.

He battered them with huge hailstones.

He sent millions of locusts to destroy their crops.

He covered all of Egypt in darkness.

Finally God took the life of the eldest boy in every Egyptian family, even Pharaoh's. Now Pharaoh listened. He told Moses to take the Israelites out of his land, out of Egypt.

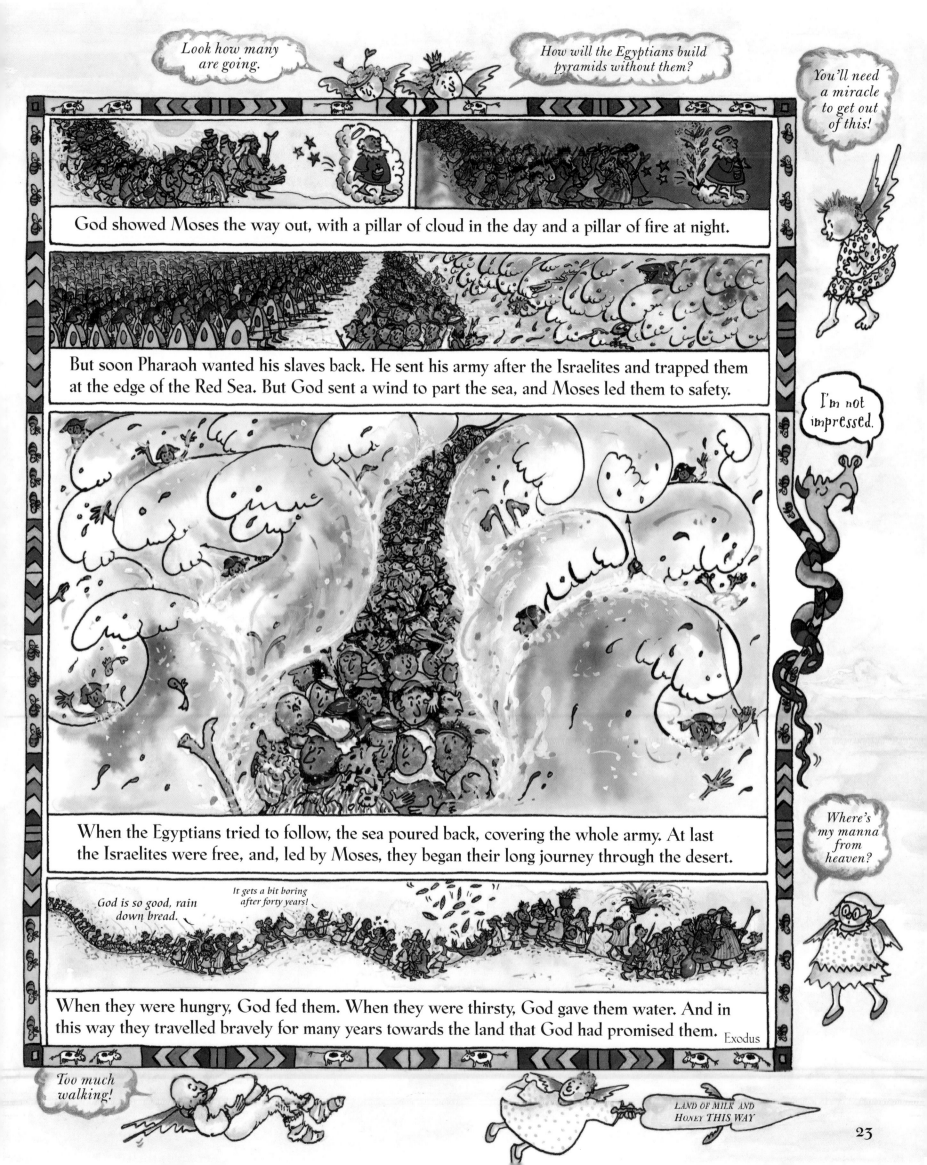

God showed Moses the way out, with a pillar of cloud in the day and a pillar of fire at night.

But soon Pharaoh wanted his slaves back. He sent his army after the Israelites and trapped them at the edge of the Red Sea. But God sent a wind to part the sea, and Moses led them to safety.

When the Egyptians tried to follow, the sea poured back, covering the whole army. At last the Israelites were free, and, led by Moses, they began their long journey through the desert.

When they were hungry, God fed them. When they were thirsty, God gave them water. And in this way they travelled bravely for many years towards the land that God had promised them. Exodus

It's so exciting, they've reached their land.

Take a deep breath before you shout.

THE LORD'S ARMY

By the time the Israelites reached the River Jordan, Moses was too old to travel further. So God gave them a new leader, a soldier named Joshua. God sent an angel to tell Joshua how to destroy the city of Jericho, which stood between the Israelites and their Promised Land. Once a day for six days Joshua marched his army in silence around the walls of Jericho. Seven priests went with them, sounding their trumpets and carrying the golden ark that held the ten commandments which God had given to Moses.

They say soldiers starve on army rations.

No shouting yet?

Spoilsport!

24

On the seventh day the procession marched around the closed city seven times. On the seventh time, when the priests gave one long trumpet blast, the soldiers all gave a great war cry – and the walls of Jericho collapsed before them. Then the soldiers charged in and burned the whole city and everything in it. God was with Joshua and the Israelites that day, and their fame spread far and wide. Now they were free to live in the land He had promised to Moses so long ago.

Joshua

After the fall of Jericho the Israelites settled in the Promised Land. But they had to fight to keep it, and sometimes they lost and were ruled over by other nations, such as the Philistines.

But God sent numerous leaders to help the Israelites. And the strongest was Samson. He once killed a thousand Philistine soldiers with just the jawbone of a donkey.

The Philistines feared Samson and wanted to know how he could be subdued, so they bribed Delilah, his love, to find out.

Delilah cajoled Samson into telling her that being tied by seven green thongs would weaken him – but it did not.

After more cajoling, Samson said that weaving his hair would weaken him – but it did not.

Delilah became so angry that Samson decided he had better tell her the truth!

26

That night a Philistine shaved Samson's head. As his hair fell about the bed, his strength left him.

The cruel Philistines blinded Samson and set him to work in a lonely prison.

Months later, the Philistine rulers gathered in their temple and called for Samson. They planned to taunt him. But Samson's hair had grown again and he asked the jailer to stand him near two pillars. Calling upon God's help, he pushed against the pillars with all his might until the temple came down, burying all the people in it. And so Samson died with his enemies.

Judges

27

DAVID AND GOLIATH

The Israelites had many leaders, but no king except God. Until they crowned Saul.

King Saul was to help them fight the Philistines and their giant warrior, Goliath.

The fearful Goliath challenged King Saul to find a soldier to fight him in single combat.

King Saul offered many fine rewards, but no Israelite dared to fight the giant.

For forty days and forty nights Goliath took his stand, but still no soldier volunteered.

David, a shepherd boy, heard Goliath's challenge while taking food to his soldier brothers.

David was enraged. Goliath's challenge was an insult to God. So he offered to fight.

Although David was only a boy, King Saul gave him his own armour and sent him forth.

David found the armour too heavy and threw it off.

God's creatures have no sense!

MMMM!

Nobles after my own heart!

Daniel was an Israelite from a noble family. When the Babylonians besieged the city of Jerusalem, they seized treasure and took Daniel and three other young nobles to Babylon to serve their king. The Babylonians did not believe in God. They honoured their own gods and goddesses.

Daniel and his friends were offered rich food and wine.

But they kept God's law and only ate simple food.

They were wise young men and soon became royal counsellors.

God had made Daniel the wisest.

So King Darius made him a state governor.

The Babylonian nobles were outraged!

They plotted to dishonour Daniel.

They persuaded the king to say that everyone had to worship him or else be fed to the lions.

As the Babylonian nobles had hoped, Daniel would only worship his God.

The delighted nobles rushed to inform the king and demand Daniel's punishment.

30

You have no heart!

But I have a very large heart.

King Darius loved Daniel, but he had to uphold the law of his kingdom. Daniel was thrown into the lions' den. King Darius spent a sleepless night imagining his friend being eaten by the lions.

At the first light of dawn he ran to the den and called out to Daniel. To his amazement, Daniel answered. With the help of an angel, God had shut the mouths of the lions.

The king was overjoyed and declared that all Babylonians should now honour the God of Daniel. The nobles were not pleased.

JONAH AND THE GREAT FISH

Go to the great city of Nineveh and preach against it.

Nineveh ... me? You're joking? You're not joking!

I'd go to Nineveh for you!

Too high again.

God wanted people to be kind; when they were cruel he tried to change their ways. He once asked the prophet Jonah to go to Nineveh in Assyria and warn the people against their wickedness.

Ahoy, hold-hard, heave over ... WAIT!

You'll be for it now!

Assyria was the land of Israel's enemy, and Jonah did not want to go. He hurried aboard a ship sailing in the opposite direction. This angered God!

So God sent a terrifying storm that threatened to break up the ship. The wind tore at its sails and the waves crashed against its hull. The ship shuddered and creaked.

He is seriously angry.

Sssplendid! A disobedient prophet.

Jonah prayed to God, but the waves grew taller and more violent. Jonah told the sailors that God had sent the storm because he had not obeyed Him.

Jonah asked the sailors to throw him into the sea, then God would calm the waters. But they did not want to drown Jonah, so they tried hard to row to land. But the sea was too wild.

Eventually the sailors were forced to throw Jonah overboard. The waters grew calm.

While the sailors rowed towards land, Jonah sank beneath the surface of the sea.

Jonah did not drown, because God sent a great fish to swallow him. He stayed inside the belly of the fish for three days and three nights, praying for God's forgiveness.

Then God told the fish to vomit Jonah out onto dry land. God again asked Jonah to go to Nineveh and warn the people against their wickedness. This time Jonah went!

In Nineveh, Jonah warned the people that God would destroy their city unless they repented.

The king and Ninevites believed Jonah. They put on sackcloth and turned their backs on evil.

When God saw that Jonah had changed the minds of the Ninevites He decided to spare Nineveh. Everyone rejoiced and praised God. And God was happy with His creations.

Jonah

Goodnight!

WALKER BOOKS is the world's leading
independent publisher of children's books.
Working with the best authors and illustrators
we create books for all ages, from babies
to teenagers – books your child will
grow up with and always remember. So…

FOR THE BEST CHILDREN'S BOOKS,
LOOK FOR THE BEAR